DISC

VAMPIRES
AND OTHER BLOODSUCKERS

by Ruth Owen

Consultant: Troy Taylor
President of the American Ghost Society

BEARPORT
PUBLISHING

New York, New York

Credits

Cover and Title Page, © Unholy Vault Designs/Shutterstock and © Isabell Schatz/Shutterstock; 4–5, © Kim Jones; 6–7, © Rechitan Sorin/Shutterstock, © Antony McAulay/Shutterstock, and © bds/Shutterstock; 8, © Fer Gregory/Shutterstock; 8–9, © William Attard McCarthy/Shutterstock; 10, © CLM/Shutterstock; 11, © Nikolay Doychinov/Getty Images; 13, © Kiselev Andrey Valerevich/Shutterstock, © zhu difeng/Shutterstock, © AF Archive/Alamy, and © Allard One/Shutterstock; 15, © Unholy Vault Designs/Shutterstock and © Teresa Yeh/Shutterstock; 16–17, © AF Archive/Alamy; 18, © iStockphoto; 18–19, © Tamara Kulikova/Shutterstock; 19, © Alex Mit/Shutterstock; 20, © Bettmann/Corbis; 21, © AlamyCelebrity/Alamy; 22, © Prisma Archivo/Alamy; 23, © Everett Collection/Rex Features; 25, © AF Archive/Alamy; 26, © Patricia Fogden/Minden Pictures/FLPA; 27, © Lions Gate/Everett Collection/Rex Features; 28L, © YorkBerlin/Shutterstock and © Sebastian Kaulitzki/Shutterstock; 28R, © Potapov Alexander/Shutterstock; 29TL, © Hintau Aliaksei/Shutterstock and © Delmas Lehman/Shutterstock; 29TR, © Linda Bucklin/Shutterstock and © Jason Patrick Ross/Shutterstock; 29B, © Brian Chase/Shutterstock.

Publisher: Kenn Goin
Senior Editor: Joyce Tavolacci
Creative Director: Spencer Brinker
Design: Emma Randall
Editor: Mark J. Sachner
Photo Researcher: Ruby Tuesday Books Ltd

Library of Congress Cataloging-in-Publication Data

Owen, Ruth, 1967–
  Vampires and other bloodsuckers / by Ruth Owen.
      p. cm. (Not Near Normal: the paranormal)
  Includes bibliographical references and index.
  ISBN 978-1-61772-722-1 (library binding) — ISBN 1-61772-722-9 (library binding)
  1. Vampires. I. Title.
  GR830.V3094 2013
  398.21—dc23
                                        2012042198

For more information, write to Bearport Publishing Company, Inc., 45 West 21st Street, Suite 3B, New York, New York 10010. Printed in the United States of America.

10 9 8 7 6 5 4 3 2 1

Contents

A Vampire's Heart

On a cold January night in 2004, six men crept into a dark cemetery on the outskirts of Marotinu de Sus, a tiny village in southern Romania. The men carried shovels, a **pitchfork**, and a razor-sharp **scythe**.

The men carefully walked between the crumbling **tombstones** until they reached the grave of a family member, Petre Toma. Together, the men began to dig until they had uncovered Toma's coffin. After opening the coffin's lid, one of the men slashed Toma's chest wide open with the scythe. Another man plunged the pitchfork into Toma's heart, pulling it out of his **corpse**.

Then the men built a fire nearby and lowered the bloody heart into the flames. As the heart burned, the men felt no regret at what they had just done. They believed burning Petre Toma's heart was the only way to protect their family and village from what he had become—a vicious, bloodthirsty **vampire**.

A Family Dinner

In Romania, vampires are known as *strigoi*. According to **legend**, a *strigoi* is a dead body that comes back to life to feed on the blood of the living. The creature climbs from its grave at night and visits family members to suck their blood as they sleep.

Petre Toma
1927-2003

Petre Toma, the Vampire?

Why did Petre Toma's family think he was a vampire? Just before Christmas 2003, 76-year-old Petre Toma died. His body was buried in the village cemetery. Soon after Toma's death, his niece became seriously ill. The weak and **feverish** young woman told her family that a *strigoi*, or vampire, was visiting her at night to drink her blood. The vampire, she said, was her dead uncle—Petre Toma.

The family believed that the only way to save the young woman's life was to destroy the blood-sucking vampire and burn his heart. So, on that January night in 2004, the men from Toma's family dug up his body, tore out his heart, and then set it ablaze.

As Petre Toma's heart burned, the men gathered ashes from the fire. They blended the ashes with water and fed the mixture to Toma's niece. By the following morning, the young woman felt well again—the vampire's **reign of terror** was over!

Vampire Hunters

In **folktales** from Eastern Europe, vampire hunters called *dhampirs* were paid to rid a village of the bloodthirsty creatures. According to legend, a *dhampir* was the child of a human mother and a vampire father, who could detect and destroy vampires.

Back from the Dead

It seems incredible that anyone would believe a family member had become a vampire. However, in Romania and other parts of Eastern Europe, many people think these creatures really exist. Why? For hundreds of years, people have passed down stories of vampires.

According to legend, these creatures sleep in their graves by day. If a person were to open a vampire's coffin in the daytime, the body inside would show no signs of **decay**—as if it were still alive. If the vampire had been feeding, its body would be **bloated** with its victims' blood. As a result, its skin might be deep purple or red in color. Often, a telltale dribble of blood would be trickling from the creature's lips. At night, however, vampires must leave their resting places to feed on the blood of the living.

Hair and Nails

In some vampire stories, a corpse may have been in its grave for months, but its hair and nails appear to have kept growing. This may be a sign that the body is not really dead but has returned to life as a vampire.

Becoming a Vampire

Why would a dead body leave its grave to become a blood-sucking *strigoi*? Some stories say that a person might become a vampire if he or she was dishonest, cruel, or violent while alive. People who practiced **witchcraft** might also **transform** into bloodthirsty monsters.

In parts of Romania, some people take gruesome **precautions** to prevent the dead from becoming vampires. Legend says that one way to stop a corpse from changing into a vampire is to thrust a silver needle through its heart before it is buried.

Other old **customs** describe ways to stop a dead body from leaving its grave if it were to become a vampire. Sometimes, the **tendons** in a corpse's knees were cut to prevent it from walking. Or, in other cases, an iron **stake** was pounded through the corpse's heart and deep into the ground. This would keep the body from leaving its grave.

silver needle

No Escape!

Old folktales say that a corpse should be buried facedown. Then, if the dead body becomes a vampire and tries to dig out of its grave, the creature will only dig farther down into the earth.

This 700-year-old skeleton was discovered in eastern Europe. It has a thick, iron stake piercing its chest where its heart would have been.

iron stake

Bloody Fangs

Over the centuries, the fear of vampires spread from Eastern Europe to other parts of the world. Terrifying stories were told of vampires living alongside humans. Unlike the bloated, bloody *strigoi* of Romanian legends, these deadly creatures might look like very attractive humans.

Like *strigoi*, however, these modern-day vampires also need to drink blood to survive. When it's time to feed, they part their lips to reveal pointed, white fangs. The sharp teeth are used to pierce the flesh of their victims.

These vampires are also thought to have **supernatural** skills. Some are able to fly. Others can climb up buildings with ease, seemingly able to stick to surfaces like an insect. They are also believed to be 20 times stronger than a human.

Sleeping In

According to some stories, a vampire's skin will burn if it is exposed to sunlight. During the day, therefore, most vampires sleep in a dark place, such as inside a coffin or tomb. When the sun sets, these creatures of the night wake up and are ready to hunt.

Time to Feed

What does it feel like to live as a vampire? No one knows for sure, but according to stories, a vampire might describe it like this:

A Vampire's Diary

The sun sets and I awake as I have done every night for more than 400 years. Like all vampires, it is my fate to never grow old.

I float through the night as a cloud of mist and enter my victim's home through a tiny crack.

I return to my human form and sink my fangs into the neck of my sleeping victim. As I feed, the terrified young woman awakens.

Tomorrow morning, the poor creature's strength will be fading. By then, I will be many miles away, sleeping soundly in my dark tomb.

Becoming a Vampire

In some stories, a person who has been bitten by a vampire may also become a vampire. In order to become one of the undead, however, the victim must first drink the blood of his or her attacker.

Vampires Among Us

A vampire may live alone or in a group known as a nest. Vampires in a nest may share a home or live together in the same neighborhood as humans.

If vampires are living among us, what are some signs that a neighborhood family is really a bloodthirsty nest of vampires? One important clue is that the creatures are never seen outside in daylight. Also, according to legend, if a vampire stands in front of a mirror, it will have no reflection. Some stories say that vampires also cast no shadow.

Vampire Regents

A vampire nest is usually controlled by a powerful, **elder** vampire known as a vampire regent. A vampire regent may be hundreds of years old and has the power to change into an animal such as a bat, a rat, or a wolf.

A vampire transforms into a horrifying bat-like creature.

Keep Out!

If a vampire is living nearby, how can people remain safe? It's important to remember that a vampire cannot enter a person's home unless invited. So if there's a knock at the door, first check to see who's there. After the vampire has been invited in, it can then return—with no invitation needed. Once inside, it will feast on the people sleeping in the house!

One way, it is said, to keep a vampire away is to put lots of garlic around doors and windows. It's also a good idea to carry a **crucifix** and some **holy water**. The cross is a powerful symbol of good. A vampire that sees a crucifix will back away in terror. If holy water is thrown on the evil creature, the water will burn its skin.

crucifix

garlic

No Vampires Allowed

A vampire cannot walk on ground that is holy, such as in a church or a temple. Also, the creature is not able to cross a stream, river, or anyplace where there is running water.

Goodbye, Bloodsuckers

While people may try to protect themselves against a vampire, ultimately the creature has to be destroyed. Cutting out and burning a vampire's heart is just one way to kill it. According to some legends, the best weapons for destroying a vampire are a wooden stake or a knife with a silver blade.

What's the most effective way to kill a vampire with a stake or knife? As the creature sleeps during the day, the wooden stake or silver blade must be driven through its heart. Then the bloodsucker's head should be cut off. Finally, the head and body should be burned separately, and the ashes from the two fires scattered far apart.

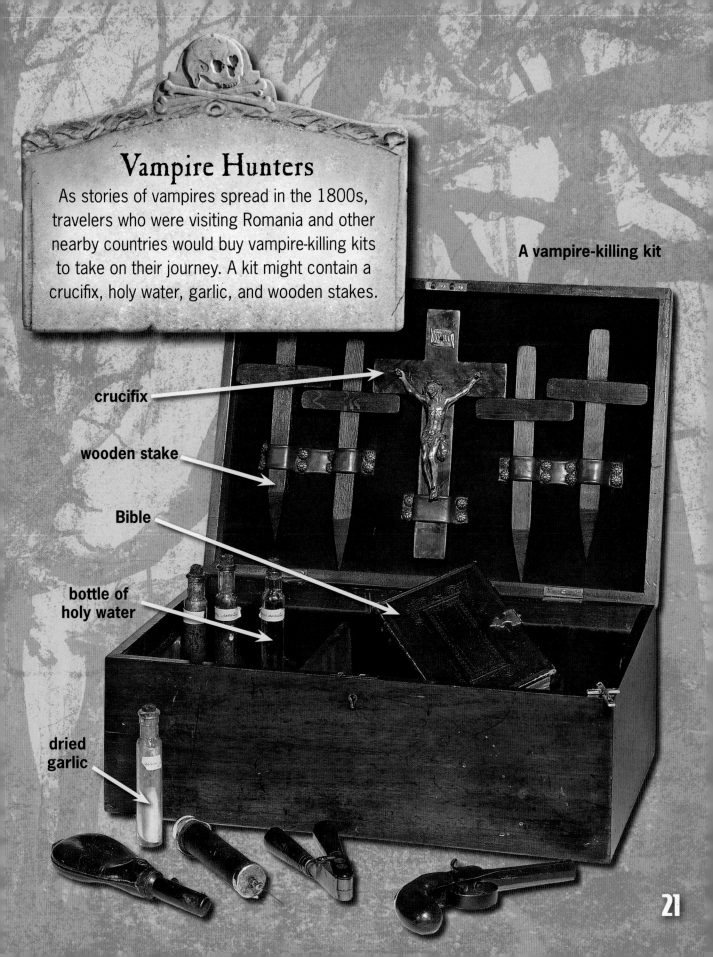

Vampire Hunters

As stories of vampires spread in the 1800s, travelers who were visiting Romania and other nearby countries would buy vampire-killing kits to take on their journey. A kit might contain a crucifix, holy water, garlic, and wooden stakes.

A vampire-killing kit

crucifix

wooden stake

Bible

bottle of holy water

dried garlic

The First Dracula

The terrifying stories of vampires that were told in Eastern Europe became the inspiration for many writers. In the late 1800s, Irish writer Bram Stoker created the most famous vampire of all time in his book *Dracula*.

Count Dracula, the name of Stoker's vampire, was inspired by a real prince. He ruled an area that is now part of Romania called Wallachia in the mid 1400s. The prince was the son of Vlad Dracul, so he was known as Vlad Dracula, which means "son of Dracul."

Vlad Dracula was not a vampire, but he was incredibly brutal. Vlad's favorite method of killing his enemies was to **impale** their bodies onto wooden spikes. Sometimes it took three days of terrible pain for his enemies to die. Vlad Dracula, or Vlad the Impaler as he was also known, may have killed up to 100,000 people by impaling them.

Vlad the Impaler surrounded by his victims

Count Dracula in the movie
Bram Stoker's Dracula

Creating a Vampire

Bram Stoker described Count Dracula as having unusually sharp, white teeth. Stoker's Dracula had hair on the palms of his hands and long, pointed fingernails. His breath was so disgusting that it could make a person feel sick.

Edward Cullen

For nearly 100 years, Dracula was the most well-known vampire in the world. This all changed, however, in 2003, when American writer Stephenie Meyer wrote a book about vampires based on a dream that she had. Her book *Twilight* introduced the world to a new vampire—Edward Cullen.

Edward Cullen was born more than 100 years ago, in 1901. However, he is forever 17, the age he was when he first became a vampire. Edward is handsome, with skin like white marble. His superhuman strength allows him to crush metal and pick up cars. He spends his life, however, trying not to hurt humans. Edward drinks the blood of animals instead.

Today, Meyer's Twilight books have sold millions of copies. The Twilight movies, which are based on the books, are also worldwide **blockbusters**.

Naming a Vampire

Stephenie Meyer chose the name Edward Cullen for her vampire because she found the name *Cullen* on English tombstones from the 1600s. In the book, Edward's adopted vampire father, Carlisle Cullen, was born in England in 1640.

twilight

Fact or Fiction?

For hundreds of years, people have believed in blood-sucking vampires. So how did these stories get started? One explanation could be that, in the past, people did not understand what happens to a dead body as it decays.

After a person dies, the body often becomes bloated because it fills with gas. Blood might also leak from the corpse. A dead person's skin may shrink and tighten. This can make fingernails and hair appear longer—as if they're still growing. When people saw these deathly changes, it's possible that they believed that corpses were still alive and sucking blood from the living.

We will never know exactly how legends about vampires began. One thing is for sure, though—people have been terrified of vampires for hundreds of years. Are our fears just imagined? Or could there be something not near normal out there—something hungry for human blood?

Real-Life Bloodsuckers

The vampire bat is a real-life bloodsucker. It uses its sharp teeth to make small slices in the skin of large animals, such as cows or horses. Then the bat laps up the animal's blood with its tongue.

A vampire hungry for blood from the movie *Daybreakers*

Vampires Around the World

Here are profiles of bloodsuckers from around the world. Check out who's who in the world of vampires and find out where in the world these horrifying creatures are likely to show up—and how they satisfy their hunger for blood.

Bramaparusha
(*brah*-mah-puh-ROO-shuh)

Location: India

Description: This male vampire rips the intestines from the bodies of humans and animals and then wears them around his neck like a necklace or on his head like a crown.

Behavior: Bramaparusha collects his victims' blood in a skull that he uses as a cup to drink from. He often eats his victims' brains and sometimes their entire bodies.

Loogaroo (LOO-*guh*-roo)

Location: Haiti and other Caribbean countries

Description: A *loogaroo* is a vampire witch that looks like an old woman during the day. At night, however, the creature removes its human skin and becomes a ball of fire.

Behavior: A *loogaroo* works for the devil. Once she has become a fireball, she flies from house to house, sucking blood from humans. She then gives the warm blood to the devil to feed on.

Upier (oop-YEER)

Location: Poland

Description: An *upier* is a dead body that has come back to life. Sometimes, this vampire has a spiked tongue that helps it tear open bodies to get as much blood as possible.

Behavior: An *upier* hunts for victims between midday and midnight. *Upiers* are very greedy for blood, drinking vast quantities of it, bathing in it, and even sleeping in pools of it.

Yara-ma-yha-who (YAH-ruh-muh-yah-hoo)

Location: Australia

Description: This vampire looks like a little red man with a large head and suckers on the ends of its fingers and toes.

Behavior: A *yara-ma-yha-who* lives in a fig tree. When a tired traveler sits beneath the shady tree to rest, the vampire climbs down from the tree and attacks. It sucks all the blood from the person's body using the suckers on its hands and feet. Then it eats its victim's bloodless corpse.

Baobhan Sith (buh-VAWN SHEE)

Location: Scotland

Description: A *Baobhan Sith* is a vampire that looks like a beautiful young woman. She usually wears a long, green dress that hides her feet, which are goat hooves.

Behavior: Groups of these beautiful vampires live in forests. When young men enter the forest, the young women ask the men to dance with them. As the couples dance, however, the vampires slash the men's bodies with their long, sharp fingernails and then drink their blood.

Glossary

bloated (BLOHT-ed) swollen with fluid or gas

blockbusters (BLOK-buhss-turz) books or movies that are very popular

corpse (KORPS) a dead body

crucifix (KROO-suh-*fikss*) a cross, often with a figure of Jesus Christ on it

customs (KUSS-tuhmz) usual ways of doing things

decay (di-KAY) rotting matter; turning into rotting matter

elder (EL-dur) older, often deserving greater respect

feverish (FEE-vur-ish) experiencing a rise in body temperature

folktales (FOHKTAYLZ) stories that are common to a certain group or culture, often passed on by word of mouth

holy water (HOHL-ee WAW-tur) water blessed by a priest and used in religious ceremonies

impale (im-PAYL) to drive a sharp wooden pole or stake through a person's body

legend (LEJ-uhnd) a story handed down from long ago that is often based on some facts but cannot be proven true

pitchfork (PICH-fork) a farm tool with a long handle and sharp metal points

precautions (pree-KAW-shunz) things done in advance to prevent something dangerous or unpleasant from happening

reign of terror (RAYN uhv TER-ur) a period of time in which violence occurs

scythe (SIETH) a tool with a long, curved blade

stake (STAYK) a pole with a sharp point at the end

supernatural (*soo*-pur-NACH-ur-uhl) having to do with something that breaks the laws of nature

tendons (TEN-duhnz) strong cords that join muscles to bones

tombstones (TOOM-stohnz) blocks of stone that mark graves

transform (transs-FORM) to change into something else

vampire (VAM-pire) a dead person who rises from the grave to suck the blood of the living

witchcraft (WICH-kraft) the actions or magical powers of a witch

Bibliography

The Official Website of Stephenie Meyer: *www.stepheniemeyer.com*

Summers, Montague. *Vampires and Vampirism (Dover Occult).* Mineola, NY: Dover (2005).

Vampire Research Society: *www.gothicpress.freeserve.co.uk/Vampire%20Research%20Society.htm*

Read More

Krensky, Stephen. *Vampires (Monster Chronicles).* Minneapolis, MN: Lerner (2007).

Pipe, Jim. *Vampires (Tales of Horror).* New York: Bearport (2007).

Rooney, Anne. *Vampire Castle (Crabtree Contact).* New York: Crabtree (2008).

Learn More Online

To learn more about vampires, visit
www.bearportpublishing.com/NotNearNormal

Index

About the Author

Ruth Owen has been developing, editing, and writing children's books for more than ten years. She lives in Cornwall, England, just minutes from the ocean. Ruth loves gardening and caring for her family of llamas.